Pocket
Puzzlers:
Whodunits

10 9 8 7 6 5 4 3 2

Published by Sterling Publishing Company, Inc.
387 Park Avenue South, New York, N.Y. 10016

Material in this collection was adapted from
Five-Minute Whodunits © Stan Smith
Inspector Forsooth's Whodunits © Derrick Niederman
Challenging Whodunits Puzzles © Jim Sukach
Clever Quicksolve Whodunit Puzzles © Jim Sukach

Distributed in Canada by Sterling Piublishing
c/o Canadian Manda Group, One Atlantic Avenue, Suite 105
Toronto, Ontario, Canada M6K 3E7
Distributed in Australia by Capricorn Link (Australia) Pty Ltd
P.O. Box 6651, Baulkham Hills, Business Centre, NSW 2153, Australia
Manufactured in the United States of America.

Sterling ISBN 0-8069-4991-0

Pocket Puzzlers:
Whodunits

Stan Smith

Derrick Niederman

Jim Sukach

Sterling Publishing Co., Inc. New York

Contents

The Puzzles

The Answers

Index

The Puzzles

A Quiet Morning at the Office

There can be no question of suicide," stated Cooper emphatically. "The murder weapon, a handgun with a silencer, was found immediately in front of the victim's desk, but beyond where he could have dropped it. It also had no fingerprints, and he wasn't wearing gloves."

"I agree," said Walker. "The gun, of course, was photographed and taken for evidence before we removed the body."

Inspector Matthew Walker of the Royston Police Department, Thomas P. Stanwick, and

FBI Special Agent Ryan Cooper were in the inner office of Wilson Jasper. Until he had been found shot at his desk a few hours earlier, Jasper had been a vice president of Supertech Corporation.

The reliable Sergeant Hatch entered the office and reported to Walker.

"As you can see, sir," he said, "there are only four doors out of this office. Three lead to the offices of Jasper's aides: Joseph Springer, John King, and William Farrar. Their offices also open onto the outer hallway. The fourth door, directly facing the desk, leads to the outer office, which is occupied by Ms. Pringle, Jasper's secretary, and two clerks. The windows behind Jasper's desk cannot be opened."

While listening to Hatch's report, Stanwick glanced again over the large, bloodstained desk. When he and Walker had arrived, the body had still been slumped over the blotter, which was covered with several spattered piles of financial reports, performance evaluations, and other papers. Also on the desk were a telephone console, a pen set, a calendar, a family photograph, and a few knickknacks. A personal computer rested on a side table beside the chair.

"I've finished questioning the aides," Hatch continued. "Springer said he didn't see Jasper this morning. Jasper didn't send for him, and Springer said he didn't want to disturb him while he was doing evaluations. King and Farrar also denied seeing him this morning. Neither was sent for, and Farrar was busy with quarterly reports."

"How about Ms. Pringle?" asked Walker.

"She says Jasper arrived about eight, went right into his office, and closed the door. He had a full briefcase with him, as usual. He cleaned off his desk each night and brought a caseful of papers home."

"Did he have any appointments this morning?" asked Cooper.

"None that she knew of, and no one appeared for one. He kept his schedule and to-do list to himself. In a nutshell, no one saw anyone enter or leave Jasper's office except Jasper himself, and no one heard a shot or a noise. Ms. Pringle found the body when he wouldn't answer his intercom for a call."

"Well," said Cooper with a sigh, "a Bureau team will soon be here to examine the offices more thoroughly. It may tie in with one of our current investigations. Certainly we have established that access to the inner office was exceedingly limited."

"I think we have established rather more than that," Stanwick remarked.

"Such as?"

"Such as the identity of the killer," said Stanwick quietly.

Who murdered Wilson Jasper?

The Case of
the Weeping Widow

Inspector Matthew Walker of the Royston Police stopped by the Baskerville bungalow of Thomas P. Stanwick, the amateur logician, late one afternoon.

"Very glad to see you, Matt," said Stanwick as he ushered the inspector into his living room. "I've spent the last hour browsing in Skeat's etymological dictionary, and some company is a welcome change. Some tea will be ready soon, or would you prefer a beer?"

"Just a beer, thanks," replied Walker. He lit a cheap cigar and patted Stanwick's pet labrador, Rufus. "I just dropped in to say hello and to see if you had any thoughts on the museum robbery."

Stanwick looked puzzled as he handed his friend a mug of beer. "Museum robbery?"

"Yes. A solid gold statuette of the Weeping Widow by Rudault was stolen last Saturday night from the museum at Royston State. We have in custody the three who were involved in the theft: Michael Agusto, Maureen Berry, and Richard Casey."

"Already in custody?" said Stanwick. He sat down across from Walker in his favorite armchair. "That's great, but I hardly see why you would want my opinion."

"As I say," continued Walker, "we know they were involved, but we don't know which drove the car, which acted as lookout during the robbery, and which committed the actual theft. We do know that the thief, unlike the others, was an expert lockpick, and that the thief and the driver cased the site during the week before the theft. They've each been interrogated with the polygraph, but the results are maddeningly ambiguous."

"What did they say?"

Walker leaned forward and flipped open his official notebook.

"Berry refused to talk at all," he said, "and the others made only two statements each.

"Agusto said, '1. I don't know how to pick locks. 2. Casey was the thief.'

"Casey said, '1. Berry wasn't the lookout. 2. I didn't case the museum before the theft.'

"The problem," an exasperated Walker continued, "is that our polygraph is behaving irregularly again. All we can tell is that each man made one true statement and one false statement. But we don't know which is which!"

Stanwick laughed. "You really must get your polygraph repaired one day," he said. "No, on second thought, don't—it's too much fun as it is. Based on what you've said, I can identify the thief, the lookout, and the driver for you."

Can you?

The Case of the
Three Confessors

Thomas P. Stanwick was holding court in the Royston Chess Club lounge one evening, reminiscing to friends about the previous summer.

"You've heard me speak of Knordwyn, the curious village in Northumbria," he said. "About half of the villagers always speak the truth, and the other half always lie. While I was staying a week or so at the Grey Boar Inn near the village, a valuable golden mace was stolen from the historical society's tiny museum.

"The mace was discovered two days later, hidden in a leather shop in the village. The thief had apparently stored it there temporarily. The only ones who could have done this were three workmen in the shop named Appleby, Barrows, and Connor. They were therefore arrested as suspects.

"A preliminary hearing was held before the bewigged local magistrate," Stanwick continued.

"It seemed that most of the village crowded into the little courtroom the day the three suspects were questioned. I arrived early and got a good seat behind the prosecutor's table.

"The local authorities wanted to know, of course, who had stolen the mace. They also wanted to know just when it had been stolen.

Each suspect was questioned on both points and, much to the astonishment of the court, each offered up a confession. The statements were as follows:

Appleby: 1. I stole the mace. 2. I either committed the theft alone or had Connor as an accomplice. 3. The mace was stolen either late Wednesday afternoon or Wednesday night.

Barrows: 1. I stole the mace. 2. Appleby was my accomplice. 3. The mace was stolen late Wednesday afternoon.

Connor: 1. I stole the mace. 2. Neither Appleby nor Barrows was involved in the theft. 3. The mace was stolen late Wednesday afternoon.

"Well! The prosecutor plainly didn't know what to make of this. Court procedure mandated that a decision would have to be based on the statements of the suspects and the knowledge that each was a villager and therefore either a consistent liar or a consistent truth-teller.

"At this point, I jotted down a note and passed

it to the prosecutor. As he read it, a measure of calm returned to his troubled countenance. He then stood to address the magistrate.

"'M'lud,' he said, 'I am pleased to say that it is now possible to identify who stole the article in question, and when the crime was committed.' Which, with the help of my note, he proceeded to do. Can any of you?"

Who stole the mace, and when was it stolen?

Blackmail at City Hall

The Honorable Christopher Hawkins, one of the two deputy mayors of the city of Royston, was pacing his office in uncharacteristic agitation when Inspector Matthew Walker of the police department and Thomas P. Stanwick, the amateur logician, arrived.

"There's the note, Inspector," said Hawkins, pointing to a creased piece of paper on his desk blotter. "As crude an attempt at blackmail as you've ever seen, I'll bet."

Walker and Stanwick went to the desk and read the note, which was composed with pasted words and letters cut out of a newspaper:

HAWKINS YOU BIGAMIST
PREPARE TO PAY 20K OR BE RUINED
MORE LATER

"Why would anyone call you a bigamist?" asked Walker.

Hawkins shook his head angrily.

"Some years ago," he said, "questions were

raised about the legality of my divorce from my first wife, but they have long since been put to rest. I'm not eager to have them raised again just now, but of course I won't pay anything to stop it."

"I see," said Walker. "This note arrived this morning?"

"Yes. The envelope is beside it."

Walker looked closely at the small brown envelope. It had canceled postage, no return address, and was typed:

DEPUTY MAYOR
CITY HALL
ROYSTON

"A typed envelope, in order not to attract particular attention during delivery," remarked Stanwick. "But the blackmailer didn't want to use the typewriter any more than necessary, for fear that it might later be identified. Hence the use of newpaper clippings for the note itself, and the extreme conciseness of the address, which omits the state and ZIP code."

"Quite so," replied Walker. "The cancellation

indicates that it was mailed downtown, probably at a corner box. There was enough of an address, of course, to get it here."

Stanwick turned to Hawkins. "Who delivers the outside mail to your office?"

"We have several mail clerks. The senior clerk, Hank Blair, sorts the mail in the mail room. Other clerks then deliver it to the various offices."

"Had the envelope been opened and resealed when you received it?"

"Why, no. My secretary is out sick today, so I opened my mail myself. I'm sure the envelope still had its original seal."

Walker glanced over the note again. "The fingerprint team will be here shortly," he said, "but I doubt that the blackmailer was so careless as to leave prints."

"Even before then, Matt," said Stanwick, "I think you should question this clerk, Blair, and check his typewriter. He knows something about this matter!"

Why does Stanwick suspect Blair's involvement?

A Stamp of Suspicion

Thomas P. Stanwick and Inspector Matthew Walker were chatting in the lounge of the Royston Chess Club after an arduous game.

"Any interesting cases on hand, Matt?" asked Stanwick, lighting his pipe.

Walker nodded. "A robbery case involving a stamp collector. What's driving me nuts is that I think the victim may be lying, but I can't prove it."

"Really?" Stanwick arched his eyebrows. "Please tell me about it."

"It happened, supposedly, three nights ago, in one of the mansions up on the Hill," Walker said. "The owner, Avery Manlich, says that he was awakened about 2 A.M. by a noise downstairs in his library. Grasping a baseball bat, he crept down the stairs and paused there to switch on the light to the foyer. He also called out 'Who's there?' in the direction of the library.

"To his astonishment, two men darted out of the library and ran out the front door into the night. By the time the shocked Manlich rushed to the open door, the men were gone. Only then did he go back to the library and find his safe cracked and at least ten trays of valuable stamps missing."

"Just a moment," interrupted Stanwick. "While he was at the door, did he hear any car doors slamming or an engine starting?"

"No, he didn't. The thieves escaped on foot."

"Did Manlich describe the thieves?"

"Nothing very helpful. He said the men were dressed only in black, skintight leotards, black gloves, and black ski masks. As they ran out, both had their arms full of several trays of stamps."

"And what did your investigation reveal?"

"The deadbolt lock on the front door had been sawed off, the other lock on that door had been picked, and the safe (a rather sophisticated one) had been expertly cracked. No fingerprints or other physical evidence was left, and according to Manlich, nothing but the stamps was taken. The stamps were heavily insured, of course. Neither on the grounds nor in the surrounding area have we found any discarded ski masks or other traces of the thieves."

"And on what basis do you doubt Manlich's story?"

Walker made a wry face.

"Not much more than a gut feeling, I guess," he said. "I've dealt with collectors before though, Tom. Though usually normal in all other respects, they tend to be fanatical when it comes to their collections. This guy Manlich, it seems to me, has been just a little too cool about this whole thing. Of course, it's nothing I could take to court."

"No, I suppose not," said Stanwick with a smile. "I think a more solid basis can be found, however, for your suspicions about Manlich. His story does contain a major flaw!"

What flaw did Stanwick detect in Manlich's story?

The Final Foreclosure

It was a situation that had trouble written all over it. Niles Bronson was involved in the Ocean Towers condominium in every conceivable way: He had lived there since 1992, when the building was first constructed; he managed the condo fund, which covered all the routine expenses shared by the building's inhabitants; finally, he worked at Marine Bank, which held the mortgages on many of the condominium properties.

Several of Niles's colleagues on the condo board felt that he had conflicts of interest on the various matters that came before them. Others felt that he simply held too much influence, period. So when he was found dead in his living room one late-March evening in 1996, everyone figured it was an inside job.

No murder weapon was ever recovered, despite an immediate and exhaustive search of the entire condominium complex. But the suspicion of an "inside job" was only amplified when a search of the documents in Bronson's

files revealed that three of the building's residents were facing foreclosure proceedings. That group consisted of Herman Gertner (like Bronson, a resident of Ocean Towers since its inception), real estate developer Graham Moss, and Jeff Carrington, who at one time had been a thriving restaurateur.

Each of the three men faced his own special type of financial distress. Carrington had been tracked down by his ex-wife and now faced substantial child support payments. Moss had leveraged himself to the hilt constructing an office building that was proving to be a dismal failure. And Gertner was withholding his mortgage payments until certain long-promised improvements were made to his property. Although the three men's predicaments were entirely different, what they had in common was that each had failed to meet his mortgage payments for several months. And that fact alone placed them under great scrutiny following the murder.

Actually, whoever killed Niles Bronson was

lucky not to have been unmasked right away. A Mrs. Rose Kravitz, who lived in Suite 1507, just around the corner from Bronson's Suite 1516, claimed that she had passed a strange man in the hallway as she took out the garbage late that afternoon. Ocean Towers was a fairly small, close-knit community; those on any particular floor tended to recognize those from the same floor, and this man simply didn't belong. At the time, though, Rose didn't think much about the stranger, nor did she get a good look at him. All she remembered was that he was wearing a T-shirt and some cut-off blue jeans.

That same evening, Rose had some business to discuss with Niles Bronson, and she was perplexed when he didn't answer her knock—hadn't he said he would be in? She said that she had made sure to knock at halftime of the NCAA semifinal game between UMass and Kentucky, in order not to catch him at a bad time. She could hear the TV from outside, though, and became suspicious when her repeated knocks brought nothing. She waited until the game was over, at which point she renewed her efforts and finally called building superintendent, Win Scheinblum. Scheinblum opened the door to find Bronson's body on the floor, not far from his TV set. "Tales from the Crypt" was blaring in the background. It was evident that Bronson had been stabbed, but there was no sign of any weapon. It was only then that Rose Kravitz remembered the strange man and wondered whether he might have been involved.

However, just two nights after Bronson's murder, mayhem turned to madness in the form of another tragedy at Ocean Towers. None other than Herman Gertner was found lying on the busy walkway in front of the building, having apparently fallen from his balcony. He was alive, but just barely. He remained unconscious, unable to shed any light on what had happened to him, and hopes for his recovery were dim indeed.

As you might expect, when all else failed,

Inspector Forsooth was called in to investigate. Forsooth went first to Herman Gertner's condo. He found the door to the outside balcony still open. The balcony had a three-foot-high protective metal railing, but several of its screws had come loose, and it wasn't sturdy enough to prevent the tragedy. Next came the Bronson murder scene. Nothing had been touched since the murder, except that the TV had been turned off and, of course, the body had been removed. A search for fingerprints had come up empty. Forsooth then proceeded to Graham Moss's apartment. Surprisingly, Moss was nothing short of ecstatic. He had just lined up a large accounting firm to lease several floors of his faltering office building, and he relished the thought that his financial problems might be solved after all.

When Forsooth then spoke to the security personnel at the front desk, they confirmed that all three men on the "foreclosure list" had been on the premises for most of the day of Bronson's murder. Jeff Carrington had been out that morning, but he returned at about 2:00 P.M. and they didn't see him afterwards. They did see Graham Moss, who left at about 7:00 P.M. for a dinner engagement. And Herman Gertner left at about 8:00 P.M. to go bowling.

Forsooth's final stop was to interview Jeff Carrington, whose apartment was the most splendid of them all. Carrington admitted that he had gotten caught up in a free-wheeling, free-spending lifestyle, but it was now time to reform. He was trying to work out suitable arrangements to pay child support on time, but he conceded that staying at Ocean Towers was probably out of the question. He did ask how Herman Gertner was doing, and it was Inspector Forsooth's sad duty to inform him that Gertner had not survived his fall.

On his way out, Forsooth ran into none other than Rose Kravitz, who admitted that some morbid fascination had made her decide to go out and gawk at the mark in the pavement where Gertner had landed. She also admitted that she wondered whether he might have been the man she saw on Saturday, right about the time that Niles Bronson was killed.

But Forsooth didn't think so. In fact, it didn't take long for him to realize that there had been a conspiracy to kill Niles Bronson—one that involved two of our three suspects. And he knew precisely how they worked together. Do you?

1) Who killed Niles Bronson?
2) What was the role of the accomplice?
3) Who killed Herman Gertner and why?

Inspector Forsooth Answers Your Questions

Q1–What do we know about the motive for Bronson's murder?

We have to assume that considerable ill will had built up between Bronson and one of the men being foreclosed.

Q2–Does what the man in the hallway was wearing mean anything?

Actually, it does. His attire suggests that he wasn't hiding anything on his person.

Q3–Why were the killers "lucky not to have been unmasked right away"?

All that meant is that if Rose Kravitz had gotten a better look, she might have been able to positively ID him.

Q4–Did "Tales from the Crypt" come on directly after the game, that is, on the same channel?

No, it did not. "Tales from the Crypt" was on FOX, whereas the NCAA games were on CBS.

Q5–What was the time of the fatal attack on Bronson?

Well, my previous answer actually gives something of a clue. Remember, Bronson was a big basketball fan and wouldn't have missed those games for the world.

Q6–What floor did Gertner live on?

I'm not sure of the exact floor, but there's an important inference available here, one that's quite relevant to the solution.

Q7–What kinds of repair needed to be done to Gertner's condo?

Wouldn't you know it? His balcony needed repairing. Gertner felt that it was dangerous, and it looks as though he was right.

Q8–When do they fire up the incinerator?

Well, in this day and age, Ocean Towers didn't have an incinerator. But trash disposal is a vital ingredient to this crime, that's for sure!

Q9–Why wasn't the work done on Gertner's condo?

He always felt it was because he wasn't as wealthy as some of the other occupants of the building, and therefore didn't carry as much clout.

Q10–Did it matter that Carrington's condo was the most splendid of all of them?

Actually, in a curious way, that fact is a nice little clue, once you think about the various factors that can make an oceanfront condo splendid.

Q11–Is there an exit to the building that doesn't go by the security personnel?

No, there isn't.

Q12–Was the murder weapon dropped down an incinerator shaft?

Great question! The incinerator part has already been covered, but the shaft is a great place to look. Remember, though, the garbage area in the basement was thoroughly inspected, and they didn't come up with a murder weapon.

Can you solve the mystery?

Roadblock

"Looks like somebody knew they were coming and cut this tree down to block the way so they could overcome the guards and get the money from the bank truck," Officer Longarm told Dr. J.L. Quicksolve and Sergeant Rebekah Shurshot. "I found the driver and guard tied up in the back of the armored truck," he said.

They were about five miles from town. The armored bank truck with one guard and a driver had left the downtown branch of the Bingo National Bank and Trust at six o'clock that morning. The driver and guard stood near Officer Longarm's police car, waiting to answer questions.

"The bank got a call from the driver this morning at six-thirty," Officer Longarm continued. "The driver told them about the tree down over the road. He said it didn't look like anyone was around, so they would get out and see if they could move it. The bank said they heard nothing further, so they called the police. I was just passing the bank when the message came over the radio, so I headed out this way. I got here in five minutes and found this."

Dr. Quicksolve walked around the armored truck. The doors were wide open, and it was empty. The tree that lay across the road was long enough to prevent a large vehicle from getting past. It was small enough, though, that two men might have been able to drag it out of the way.

"It's funny that the robbers would know which way the bank truck was coming," Sergeant Shurshot said. "They change their route every day."

"I think they knew as soon as the driver was told," Dr. Quicksolve said, "but they still took their time."

What did Dr. Quicksolve mean?

Suspicious Plumber

"I don't know exactly what the diamond neck-lace is worth, but my boyfriend Rod could tell you," Kitty Purring told Dr. J.L. Quicksolve and Sergeant Rebekah Shurshot as they sat in her kitchen. Kitty played nervously with a small ball of yarn as she spoke. "The plumber must have stolen it when I was taking the trash out," Kitty continued. "It was there in the drawer earlier, and I noticed it was gone a couple hours after the plumber left. I called the police right away."

"Have you known Rod for a long time?" Sergeant Shurshot asked.

"Yes, I have. You can't suspect him. I've known him a long time. Of course, he hasn't been my boyfriend that long—just since my roommate moved out."

"Your roommate?" Dr. Quicksolve asked.

"Yes, Randee Peakout. She was jealous of Rod and me. She didn't have any reason to be. She just got mad, broke up with Rod, and moved out. Rod and I started dating a little later." Kitty

sat up in her chair and pointed out the window. "She lives right there across the court. I think she spies on us out that window."

"Has Rod or anyone else been here today?" Dr. Quicksolve asked.

"No, I live alone now. Rod called this morning. That's all. After breakfast I went to rinse my dishes, and the sink was plugged up. I called a plumber right away and said I had a problem. He said someone would be here this afternoon, but the plumber got here right away. He fixed it in about 10 minutes and was gone."

"Did you know him?" Dr. Quicksolve asked.

"No, I..." Kitty was interrupted by the doorbell and went to answer it. A woman stood at the door in gray work clothes with a belt full of tools around her waist and a tool box in her hand.

Dr. Quicksolve and Sergeant Shurshot looked at each other. Dr. Quicksolve said, "Randee."

What did Dr. Quicksolve suspect?

Timing Is Everything

The case started out as a robbery but ended up as a homicide. On the face of it, that's not the strangest combination in the world. But in this case the person who was robbed wasn't the person who was murdered!

Early one Saturday morning, in the country town of Cedarville, a man named Buford Huxley reported that his tool shed had been broken into. The shed was secured by an ordinary combination lock that had been cleanly severed, probably with a pair of bolt cutters. The shed was located right outside Huxley's barn, and was where he kept all sorts of gardening tools—rakes, hoes, and the like. But most important of all was that he kept a set of hunting rifles there, and one of them was missing. That item was of particular interest to Inspector Forsooth upon his arrival that morning.

Forsooth knew something that Huxley might not have known. What Forsooth knew was that a man named James Hooligan, who lived about 30

43

minutes away, had been murdered just the night before by a rifle shot that came through the window of his home. And that set the stage for an interesting exchange.

Shortly after Forsooth arrived at Huxley's place, Muriel Huxley came out to the barn screaming, "Did you hear what happened?!" She had been listening to an all-news radio station while doing some gardening, and had heard the account of the murder. When she saw Forsooth, she backed off a bit, and he assumed it was because her hands and face were quite dirty. She apologized for her appearance, explaining that she had just finished planting some 300 daffodil bulbs along a stone wall behind their house. However, Forsooth wasn't too concerned with how she looked, because there was more to this story than met the eye.

Buford Huxley seemed strangely self-conscious upon hearing of Hooligan's death. It was clear that Hooligan was no stranger to this household, and the ties grew deeper as the investigation progressed. For one, the murder weapon was discovered in a wooded area about halfway between the Huxley and Hooligan residences. It was Huxley's missing rifle, all right, and ballistics tests confirmed that it was the source of the fatal shots. Separately, police uncovered a pair of slightly rusty bolt cutters not far from the rifle. Huxley admitted that the gun was his, but denied any part in the shooting. However, the Huxleys had to own up to some crucial and somewhat embarrassing facts upon further questioning.

According to Muriel Huxley, James Hooligan had been blackmailing her husband and two other men, Edgar Plotz and Dinky Martinez, for their participation in a kickback scheme several years before, when her husband worked for Acme Construction Company: Plotz and Martinez had given Huxley kickbacks in return for Huxley selecting their then-struggling roofing company as a major subcontractor on projects spearheaded by Acme. Buford Huxley now worked with Plotz and Martinez in their own concrete-pouring venture, and part of the

Huxley barn had been converted into an office for that venture. Hooligan had managed to figure out that the seed money for this new enterprise had come illegally.

Huxley at first denied the plot, but he conceded that he had received a threatening letter from Hooligan just days before. He also said that it was only a coincidence that the shed had been locked in the first place. He said he had gotten into an argument with his wife and obtained a lock so that she couldn't access her precious gardening tools—the rifles were the last things on his mind! He acknowledged that his two business partners were the only other people who even knew about the lock, but he was quick to add that he alone knew the combination.

The night of Hooligan's death, Huxley had held a meeting with his "co-conspirators," Plotz and Martinez. The subject, of course: what to do about the blackmailing. Plotz had arrived at 8:45; Martinez at 9:00. The meeting lasted for about an hour, with no specific plan but a lot of anger and fear all around. Huxley admitted that his two friends had talked about giving Hooligan some "concrete boots," but he didn't take their bluster very seriously. Huxley also said that he had gone back to his house after the meeting. He assumed that the others had left immediately and hadn't come back, but he admitted that he wasn't sure. However, he could confirm that the lock was quite intact when he left the meeting.

The coroner determined that James Hooligan had died sometime the prior night, but it wasn't possible to pinpoint the time of death any more than that. One potentially helpful detail came from one of Hooligan's neighbors, who had been walking her dog at about 10:30. She reported that a light was on in Hooligan's downstairs bathroom, but as she walked by, that light went off. Interestingly, Hooligan's body was found in the downstairs den, whose window was right next to the bathroom window. The shot that killed Hooligan had been fired from the outside, as evidenced by a shattered window pane and some glass fragments found in the den. When investigators arrived the next morning, the den light was still on, and the bathroom light was still off.

Dinky Martinez—who, despite his name, was a strong, stocky fellow—said he returned to his home at just before midnight, a time his wife confirmed. When asked what he did after the meeting broke up, he said that he had gone out to a neighborhood bar to shoot, er, play some pool. In fact, he had told his wife he'd been playing pool all night, to conceal the true nature of his business.

Edgar Plotz, the ringleader of the embezzlement scheme, claimed he had gone directly home after the meeting, arriving there at about 10:30. Because he lived alone, there was no one who could corroborate his story. He added that he didn't know a rifle from a bulb planter, but his lawyer cut him off before he could say more; now that the kickbacks were common knowledge, Plotz needed all the counsel he could get.

As for Huxley, he admitted that his wife was asleep when he got in after the meeting, so she couldn't vouch for him, but he insisted he didn't go anywhere.

Well, are you ready? Here are your questions:

1) Who killed James Hooligan?

2) Explain the key elements of timing in this case.

3) What was the missing piece of evidence that tied the murderer to the crime?

Inspector Forsooth
Answers Your Questions

Q1—If the murder occurred after 10:30, would that implicate Dinky Martinez?

Yes, it sure would. Everyone else seems to have alibis for that time period, with the possible exception of Buford Huxley.

Q2—What time of year did the murder take place?

Presumably it was in the late fall, because Muriel Huxley was struggling to get all her daffodil bulbs planted before the ground froze. But the precise time of year isn't important.

Q3–Was the light hit by a shot from the rifle?

No, it wasn't. The only shots went through the window of the adjacent den. But knowing why the light went out would be very helpful regarding the timing of this case. Remember the title!

Q4–Was the murder related to the embezzlement?

Only indirectly. Sorry to be vague, but that's a clue in and of itself.

Q5–Would it have been possible for Buford Huxley to have gone to Hooligan's house without his wife knowing?

Absolutely. She was sound asleep.

Q6–Could Muriel have cut the lock after the meeting ended?

No, for the same reason as the answer to #5 above.

Q7–Could Buford Huxley have cut the lock himself, to make it look as though someone was framing him?

It is entirely possible, although there is no evidence to back that up. Wouldn't that be clever?

Q8–Was the lock the same one bought by Huxley?

Yes, it was. Great question, though.

Q9–Was the murder actually announced on the radio?

It sure was. Muriel was entirely legit.

Q10–Had Plotz ever been inside the tool shed?

It sure looks that way, judging by his comment about the rifle and the bulb planter. As for when he might have been inside, well, that's something that your supersleuth abilities should figure out.

Q11–Was the neighbor certain about the time the light went out?

Positive.

Q12–Why were the bolt cutters rusty?

Because they had been outside longer than you might have thought.

Can you solve the mystery?

The Churchill Letter

"Mrs. Bryant! It's nice to see you again. Please come in." Thomas P. Stanwick stood back from the door and waved his gray-haired visitor into his living room.

"I'm sorry to bother you again, Mr. Stanwick," said Ellen Bryant as she settled herself onto the sofa, "but you were so helpful with my earlier difficulty that I hoped you might advise me on this one."

"Certainly, if I can," replied Stanwick. Striding to the sideboard, he began to prepare a tray of fresh tea. "What's the problem?"

"A few days ago," she said, "I was visited by Stephen Faybush, the nephew of a couple I know in my neighborhood. He specializes in unusual investments."

"Indeed?" said Stanwick. He brought the tray over and poured two cups of Lapsang souchong. "Have you been looking for investment advice?"

"Well, I have a small nest egg that isn't earning much in the bank, and I may have men-

tioned this to my neighbors."

"And what sorts of investment does this Faybush promote?"

"Historical artifacts, mostly. Famous signatures and such. He says they consistently beat inflation as they rise in value over time."

"That's true—if they are genuine, that is." Stanwick settled himself near her on the sofa.

"Do you by chance have such an item in your folder there?"

"Exactly, yes." Mrs. Bryant opened a manila folder she had been carrying and extracted a letter. "It's a Churchill," she said as she handed it to Stanwick.

Stanwick held the document gingerly and gave a low whistle.

"A letter from Churchill's private secretary to a John McMasters," he murmured. "Not a name I recognize. Probably a constituent. 'Sir Winston very much appreciates the book you sent him' and so on. Dated in mid-1950. Cream-colored paper. Letterhead refers to Chartwell, Churchill's country home. The valuable bit is the handwritten inscription 'With warmest good wishes, Winston S. Churchill' along the bottom after the secretary's signature. Only about a year and a half later, he returned to power as Prime Minister."

"Stephen is urging me to buy it," said Mrs. Bryant. "He is letting me keep it and look it over this week."

Stanwick smiled faintly.

"My advice," he said, "is to have nothing more to do with Mr. Faybush. In fact, I think I'll place a call to the local constabulary about him. This letter is a fraud. May I suggest that you find a good mutual fund for your money?"

How does Stanwick know the letter is a fraud?

Stanwick Visits the Golden Crown

Most of the usual crowd was at the Golden Crown pub that mild summer evening. Also present was Thomas P. Stanwick, the amateur logician, who was vacationing in England again. He had just won a game of darts, and was back at his small table nursing a pint of light ale.

"Thanks for the game, Jeff," he said to his opponent. "The last shot was just dumb luck."

"You played well, Tom," replied Jeff. "It's too bad Warren Johansen can't be here tonight, though. He could give you a game."

"Indeed he could," said the publican. "His left arm is as keen with a dart as Robin Hood's bow was with an arrow."

"Well, perhaps I'll have the pleasure of meeting him tomorrow night," said Stanwick.

"I think not," said the barmaid. "He's been arrested, you know, for the burglary last weekend at the Ferrars house."

Stanwick arched his eyebrows. "Indeed? Why?"

"The glove, sir," the barmaid continued. "The safe in the den was cracked, and delicate work it was too, the constable said. Beside the safe they found a thick right glove of the kind that Warren wears in winter. And it had his initials in it! The burglar was interrupted by the return home of Mr. Ferrars, you see, and had to flee. The safe door was left open, and the jewels were gone, but there was his glove."

"Any fingerprints?" asked Stanwick.

"None," said Walter Griffin, a local shopkeeper. "The burglar had wiped the lock clean after opening the safe. Fresh footmarks on the carpet were made by a man a little over six feet tall, the constable said, which is Warren's height."

"Hmmm." Stanwick finished his mug of ale. "I would say that the case against this Johansen has a critical flaw. I'll drop by the station in the morning and, if the authorities are reasonable, I may get to play darts with the expert tomorrow evening after all."

Why does Stanwick think Johansen is innocent?

The Case of the Dubious Drowning

"A drowning at Duncomb residence, 857 Whippoorwill Drive. Victim middle-aged woman. Ambulance and unit en route."

Inspector Matt Walker and Thomas P. Stanwick listened intently to the terse announcement on Walker's police radio. Whippoorwill Drive was only minutes away, so without a word Walker, who was giving Stanwick a ride home, turned his car toward it.

The ambulance and a police car arrived just before them. Walker and Stanwick followed the commotion to the swimming pool, about 60 feet in back of the formidable Duncomb mansion. The emergency crew had just pulled Marjorie Duncomb from the pool and was trying to revive her. A moment later they hoisted her, still dripping in her swimsuit, onto a stretcher and rushed her to the ambulance.

"No life signs, sir," one medical technician said to Walker as he hurried past. Walker turned to the two police officers and a disheveled, gray-ing man standing by the pool.

"Mr. Duncomb?" he asked, flashing his badge. "Did you call this in?"

"Yes," replied the disheveled man, still staring toward the departing ambulance. "I found Marjorie face-down in the pool. The poor dear must have had a heart attack during her swim and drowned."

"Were you looking for her?"

"Yes. I knew she was late getting back from her swim. It was after three."

"Did she swim every day, then?"

"That's right. Even now, in October. It's getting chilly, though, so we were going to close up the pool for the season next week. Only next week!"

Stanwick glanced around. The pool was well maintained, but the furnishings were few: three lounge chairs and a small table. A pair of sandals lay beside one of the chairs, and a book and a pair of sunglasses lay on the table.

"Did your wife have a weak heart, Mr. Duncomb?" asked Stanwick.

"Just a bit of angina, but she took medication for it. Poor dear!"

"Matt," said Stanwick quietly, drawing Walker aside. "If Mrs. Duncomb cannot be revived, will an autopsy be required?"

"Of course."

"Well, I think you will find little or no water in her lungs. This is wrong. She didn't drown. She died elsewhere and was moved to the pool, which indicates murder. Until the autopsy results are in, I think you had better keep an eye on the husband."

Why does Stanwick suspect that Mrs. Duncomb was murdered?

Stanwick and the
Spurious Silver Miner

"And how can I help you, Mr. ... Lancaster?"

"Lanchester, Garver Lanchester. Just up from southern Brazil, and delighted to be visiting New England."

Thomas P. Stanwick, the amateur logician, lit his curved briar and looked curiously at the visitor seated in the opposite armchair whose unexpected appearance had interrupted his researches into ancient geometrical studies. Lanchester, a large, mustachioed man, wore a trace of an Australian accent and, despite the February cold, the light khakis of an explorer.

"Inspector Walker has given me a letter of introduction," Lanchester said, handing Stanwick a sealed envelope. "He told me you had some millions to invest, despite your modest lifestyle, as he put it, sir."

Stanwick froze in astonishment for a second before taking and opening the envelope. Inside he found a slip of paper with a few lines of

Walker's distinctive handwriting:

> Sorry to tell fibs about you, Tom, but
> I thought you'd find Mr. Lanchester's
> story as interesting as I did.
>
> Matt

"Please proceed, Mr. Lanchester," said Stanwick, leaning back in his chair and smiling expectantly.

"Well, sir," Lanchester began, "I've spent the better part of my life prospecting for precious metals in some of the more remote areas of the world. China, Mongolia, northern Canada, Siberia, the jungles of Southeast Asia, as well as the outback of my native Australia, have all felt the mark of my pick and shovel.

"Five weeks ago, I found myself in the hill country of southern Brazil, just north of Porte Alegre. I had heard legends of old silver mines in that area. Well, by Gawd, sir, they were true! A cluster of caves I discovered there show strong signs of rich deposits of silver. I've filed the proper papers with the Brazilian authorities. My next step is to organize a team to excavate the mines properly.

"That's where I need investors like yourself, sir. We'll need fuel, jeeps, mining equipment, tents, food—enough for several weeks. If the mines are deep enough, I can set up a permanent organization."

"And if you find the investors you need, how soon do you propose to return to the mines?"

"Immediately, sir!"

"Hadn't you better wait until summer?"

"No, sir, I'm ready to start now!"

Stanwick laughed heartily. "I'm afraid I can't help you, Mr. Lanchester, or whatever your name really is. My hidden millions are as much a fantasy as your Brazilian silver mines, as Matt Walker is well aware. Begone now, sir!"

Why doesn't Stanwick believe his visitor's story?

A Theft at the Art Museum

The theft of several valuable paintings from the Royston Art Museum created a sensation throughout New England. Two days after Stanwick's return from a visit to Scotland, he was visited by Inspector Matt Walker, who was in charge of the case. As Stanwick poured tea, Walker quickly brought his friend up to date on the case.

"We've identified the gang of five thieves who must have done this job," Walker reported. "Archie McOrr, who never finished high school, is married to another one of the five, Charlayne Trumbull. The other three are Beverly Cuttle, Ed Browning, and Douglas Stephens."

"I thought you told me earlier that only four people were involved in the robbery," said Stanwick.

"That's right. One stayed in the car as the driver, another waited outside and acted as lookout, and two others entered the museum and carried out the actual theft. One of the five gang members was not involved in this particular job at all."

"And the question, I hope," said Stanwick with a smile, "is who played what part, if any, in the theft."

"Exactly." Walker flipped open his notebook. "Though I'm glad to say that our investigation is already bearing some fruit. For example, we have good reason to believe that the lookout has a Ph.D. in art history, and that the driver was first arrested less than two years ago."

"A remarkable combination," Stanwick chuckled.

"Yes, indeed. We know that Douglas was on the scene during the robbery. One of the actual thieves (who entered the museum) is the sister of Ed Browning. The other thief is either Archie or his wife."

66

"What else do you have on Douglas?" asked Stanwick.

"Not much. Although he's never learned to drive, he used to be a security guard at the Metropolitan Museum of Art in New York."

"Interesting. Please go on."

"The rest is mainly odds and ends." Walker thumbed through a few more pages of notes. "Charlayne, an only child, is very talented on the saxophone. Beverly and Ed both have criminal records stretching back a decade or more. We've also learned that the driver has a brother who is not a member of the gang."

"Most interesting indeed," remarked Stanwick. He handed Walker a mug of tea and sat down with his own. "Your investigation has made excellent progress. So much, in fact, that you already have enough to tell who the thieves, the lookout, and the driver are."

Who are they?

A Mere Matter of Deduction

Thomas P. Stanwick, the amateur logician, removed a pile of papers from the extra chair and sat down. His friend Inspector Matthew Walker had just returned to his office from the interrogation room, and Stanwick thought he looked unusually weary.

"I'm glad you dropped by, Tom," said Walker. "We have a difficult case on hand. Several thousand dollars' worth of jewelry was stolen from Hoffman's Jewel Palace yesterday morning. From some clues at the scene and a few handy tips, we have it narrowed down to three suspects: Addington, Burke, and Chatham. We know that at least one of them was involved, and possibly more than one."

"Burke has been suspected in several other cases, hasn't he?" asked Stanwick as he filled his pipe.

"Yes, he has," Walker replied, "but we haven't been able to nail him yet. The other two are small potatoes, so what we really want to know

is whether Burke was involved in this one."

"What have you learned about the three of them?"

"Not too much. Addington and Burke were definitely here in the city yesterday. Chatham may not have been. Addington never works alone, and carries a snub-nosed revolver. Chatham always uses an accomplice, and he was seen lurking in the area last week. He also refuses to work with Addington, who he says once set him up."

"Quite a ragamuffin crew!" Stanwick laughed. "Based on what you've said, it's not too hard to deduce whether Burke was involved."

Was Burke involved or not?

The Prints of Lightness

After it was all over, the workmen outside Oscar Delahanty's home could barely comprehend the irony of what had just taken place. The men had arrived promptly at 8:30 one summer morning to install a roadside fire hydrant some fifty feet or so from Delahanty's front walkway. Barely an hour into their job, well before the new hydrant was operational, they saw smoke billowing out of a first-floor window. They contacted their buddies at the fire department, who got down as quickly as they could. However, by the time the firefighters arrived, Delahanty's small but historic home had already sustained significant damage. And that wasn't all.

When the firemen on the scene trudged upstairs to Delahanty's bedroom, they found him lying in bed, quite dead. He was still dressed in his blue silk pajamas, so clearly he hadn't enjoyed much of this sultry summer morning. The fire itself hadn't reached the upstairs, but there was plenty of smoke all around. The firemen couldn't help but notice that the window in his bedroom, which looked out onto the road, was firmly shut.

The blaze had apparently started near the back door, which was part of the "newer" section of the house. By the looks of things, the hardwood floors in that area, including the back staircase, had just been refinished, but they had been almost completely torched by the blaze. Officials couldn't be certain just what had been used to ignite the fire, but they doubted that it had started by accident.

The fire chief noted that everything in the house seemed to be in compliance with local regulations. However, he couldn't help but note that older houses were notoriously poor fire risks, and an alarm system that was directly wired into the fire department would have saved time and prevented some of the damage they were witnessing. Implicit in his remark was that a better system might have saved Delahanty's life.

The next step was to alert Delahanty's employees at The Clip Joint, the hair salon he had owned and operated for just over six years. When the authorities got there, they could see that it was a busy morning, rendered all the busier by the boss's no-show. The three stylists on the job were Ginger LaCroix, Stan Norton, and Mitchell Quinn, each of whom had worked for Delahanty since the salon opened. When told that their boss had died of asphyxia, all three were momentarily speechless. After this stunned silence was over, Quinn said he would phone the boss's other appointments and officially cancel them. Ginger LaCroix had already placed a call to Delahanty's home, but had gotten only his answering machine. She asked if the house was damaged in the fire, and expressed relief that it could probably be rebuilt. As for Stan Norton, he had apparently been planning on visiting the boss's home himself to see what was wrong, but now he did not have to.

The investigators took careful note of these various reactions, but it wasn't until 24 hours had elapsed that a possible motive appeared. A woman named Hilda Graylock came forward to say that Delahanty had offered her a job as a stylist with his salon. He indicated to her that he was planning on letting one of his staff go, but she didn't know which one. To make matters even more interesting, not long after Graylock gave her testimony, another woman appeared at the police station and gave the exact same story! These tidbits certainly changed the complexion of things, and, upon consultation with the medical examiner, police now concluded definitively that Delahanty had been murdered.

Upon returning to the salon, the authorities picked up some more information about what happened that morning. Mitchell Quinn testified that he had opened up the salon at 8:00 A.M. It was The Clip Joint's policy to rotate the responsibility for the 8:00 shift; the rest of the staff would come in later in the morning, well in time for the lunchtime crunch. The salon stayed open until 8:30 at night, and the bulk of its business was conducted at lunchtime and during the evening hours.

As it happened, everyone had worked late the night before Delahanty's death. LaCroix and Norton had gone out for a drink and a bite to eat afterwards; they were joined by a couple from the massage studio located right next to The Clip Joint. That little gathering didn't break up until about midnight, whereupon everybody went home. As for the next morning, LaCroix had come in about 9:30, while Norton had arrived at a couple of minutes past ten, something of an annoyance to his 10:00 appointment.

A revisiting of the crime scene offered a couple of important details. Ordinarily, the back door to Delahanty's home would have been locked with a deadbolt, which was of course activated from the inside. But whoever had done the floorwork had exited that way, and was unable to lock the door on the way out! So that explained how the killer could have entered the home without forced entry and without the workmen seeing him or her. Because of the layout of the house, it would have been quite easy for someone to have entered the back way without being spotted.

Upon hearing this crucial piece of information, Hilda Graylock lamented Delahanty's bad luck. He had evidently sought permission from the town clerk's office for several months to get the floors redone. (Because much of the house dated back to the early 18th century, it had attained landmark status, so he couldn't do much without the town's approval.) However, the "newer" wing, although still a century old, did not have quite the same restrictions, so the work was approved, as long as the wood was stained in a manner consistent with the rest of the woodwork. And just a day after the work was complete, Delahanty was dead.

Before the authorities could get around to identifying the murderer, they received more than they could possibly have hoped for—a confession. That's right, one of Delahanty's employees admitted to having killed the boss. Ordinarily the investigation might have ended right then and there, but in this case police truly got too much of a good thing. Later that same day, another Clip Joint employee admitted to having killed Delahanty! Neither confession could be readily dismissed. In fact, both people took lie detector tests, and they each passed with flying colors.

The bad news was that some important evidence had been destroyed. The good news was that the coroner's report turned out to invalidate one of the two confessions. Even without seeing that report, do you know who the real murderer was? Well, it's not easy, and a couple of issues will have to be resolved in the question-and-answer session that follows. But here are the questions you must answer:

1) Who killed Oscar Delahanty?

2) Who wrongly confessed to the crime?

3) How did the coroner's report help identify the killer?

4) What was the "evidence" that was destroyed?

Inspector Forsooth
Answers Your Questions

Q1–Could Ginger or Stan have killed him the prior night?

No. The folks at the massage studio could attest to their whereabouts all night.

Q2–Why is it important that Delahanty lived in a landmark house?

Because it wouldn't have been possible for him to have central air conditioning. (The fact that his bedroom window was closed suggests that there was no room air conditioner either.)

Q3–Since more than one person was being hired, does that mean that more than one person was being fired?

It certainly looks that way.

Q4–Did the floor refinishers leave the night before? If so, why didn't Delahanty check to make sure the doors were locked before going to bed?

The workmen had in fact left the night before, but they had essentially "painted in" the area near the back door, so Delahanty couldn't have gone in that area (i.e., to lock the door) without ruining the new finish.

Q5–Why was Ginger so concerned about the house?

Perhaps she had a sentimental streak, and didn't really like the idea of such a nice home being destroyed.

Q6–When the police said that the victim had been "asphyxiated," does that mean that he died of smoke inhalation?

Not necessarily. "Asphyxiation" technically refers to any situation where breathing is impaired, whether arising from smoke inhalation, strangulation, or whatever.

Q7–Did the house's landmark status mean that it couldn't have smoke alarms?

Not at all. In fact, it was even more important for Delahanty to have smoke alarms, precisely because antique houses are extremely flammable. And the fire chief would certainly have noticed had Delahanty's smoke alarms been absent or defective.

Q8–Why was a hydrant being installed at that particular location?

Pure chance. Presumably the town had simply decided that it needed more hydrants, and noted that there wasn't one close enough to Oscar and his neighbors. (On a personal note, Inspector Forsooth returned home one evening to find a fire hydrant installed on the road alongside his own house. It does happen!)

Q9–Did the work on the hydrant begin that day or earlier?

Great question. The answer is that the work began that very morning.

Q10–If it was a sultry morning, why were Oscar's windows closed?

Another excellent question. We can assume that Delahanty wouldn't have been able to get to sleep that night had his windows been closed.

Q11–Had the floor fully dried?

Given what we know about the weather, etc., it seems unlikely that the finish would have been perfectly dry. Some polyurethane finishes can take a full 24 hours to dry.

Q12–How many workmen does it take to install a fire hydrant?

No light bulb jokes, please. The answer is that it takes several people to do the job, primarily because they have to jackhammer through the pavement to get to the pipes.

Can you solve the mystery?

The Answers

A Quiet Morning at the Office

Jasper had cleaned off his desk the previous night, unpacked his papers only after arriving that morning, and kept his work schedule to himself. Once shot, he had slumped over his papers. Only someone who had seen him at his desk before he was shot could have known what he was working on.

Springer, however, had referred to Jasper's working on performance evaluations. He could have known this only by seeing the papers on Jasper's desk that morning before the shooting. Springer had therefore lied about not seeing Jasper that morning before the shooting, which only the killer would have had reason to do.

The Case of the Weeping Widow

If Agusto's first statement were false, then he would be the thief, and both his statements would be false. This is impossible. His first statement is therefore true and his second statement is false, so neither he nor Casey is the thief. The thief therefore is Berry.

Casey's first statement is true, so his second statement is false. He thus did case the museum before the theft, and so is either the thief or the driver. Since he isn't the thief, he is the driver. Agusto, by elimination, is the lookout.

The Case of the Three Confessors

The third statements of Barrows and Connor are identical, so they must either both be liars or both be truth-tellers. They cannot both be truth-tellers, since Connor's second statement contradicts Barrow's first statement. Therefore they are both liars.

This means that their confessions are false, and neither was involved in the theft. Since Connor's second statement is false, but Barrows was not involved, Appleby must have committed the theft alone.

Since Appleby is a truth-teller, the mace was stolen either late Wednesday afternoon or Wednesday night.

The third statements of Barrows and Connor are false, so it was not stolen late Wednesday afternoon. The mace was therefore stolen Wednesday night.

Blackmail at City Hall

The envelope was addressed only to "Deputy Mayor," and yet without even opening the envelope, Blair knew which deputy mayor to send it to.

A Stamp of Suspicion

A deadbolt lock had been sawed off, a door lockpicked, and a sophisticated safe cracked. What then became of the saw, the lockpick, and the safe-cracking tools?

No tools were left in the study, or carried in the thieves arms, or hidden on their persons (the leotards were skintight), or taken to an escape car. If Manlich's story were true, the thieves would have had to do the work with their bare hands, which was absurd.

The Final Foreclosure

1) Who killed Niles Bronson?

Graham Moss was the killer, assisted by Herman Gertner.

2) What was the role of the accomplice?

To dispose of the murder weapon. After killing Gertner, Moss put the knife in a sheath, placed the sheath in a bag, and dropped it down the trash chute to Gertner, who was waiting on his floor, several floors below, with a basket or some such receptacle to catch it. Gertner later placed the weapon in his bowling bag so he could remove it from the building without attracting suspicion. (Note that Gertner would have been most unlikely to even temporarily survive a plunge of as much as fifteen stories, so one can infer that he lived well below Niles Bronson. Jeff Carrington and Graham Moss, on the other hand, lived above Bronson.)

Why not Carrington instead of Moss? Well, note that in his journey through the condominium complex, Inspector Forsooth spoke to the security personnel in between speaking to Moss and Carrington. Why? Because Carrington lived in a penthouse apartment (hence the splendid views), which was accessed via a different elevator bank! To get to Bronson's apartment, Carrington would have had to return to the main floor—as Inspector Forsooth did—where he would have been spotted by the ever-vigilant security folks.

By the way, we know that the building had a trash chute by the fact that Rose was taking her garbage out on a Saturday afternoon (NCAA semi-final games are played on Saturdays). It would be highly unlikely for anyone to come around picking it up on a Saturday or a Sunday, and it would also be unlikely that the garbage would remain in the hallway of such an upscale building.

Note that the description of the murder scene indicates that Bronson was killed before the beginning of the basketball game(s), because his TV was still tuned to FOX ("Tales from the Crypt"), whereas it would have been on CBS had he been alive to watch the basketball. Therefore, neither Moss nor Gertner has any alibi for that time. (I suppose Moss could have changed the channel after killing Bronson to make it look as though he was killed after the games, but Rose Kravitz's intrusion eliminates that possibility.) Finally, the fact that Moss's personal fortunes were turning around is irrelevant. He didn't find out about the accounting firm moving into his building until Monday, by which time Bronson was already dead.

3) Who killed Herman Gertner and why?

Either Gertner was trying to blackmail Moss or expose him. Either way, Gertner wasn't cooperating, and Moss decided to get rid of him, too. Case closed.

Roadblock

Dr. Quicksolve suspected the driver and guard. He noticed that the driver and guard seemed to take thirty minutes to go five miles. They left at six o'clock and called about the roadblock at six-thirty. It only took Officer Longarm five minutes to get there from the bank. They had plenty of time to stop and pull the tree across the road with partners who then tied them up to make them look innocent.

Suspicious Plumber

Dr. Quicksolve figured Kitty's roommate might be angry enough to sneak into the apartment with her old key while Kitty was away or asleep and plug up the kitchen sink. She could watch out her window and see when Kitty discovered the problem and phoned a plumber. Then she had someone pose as a plumber and come right away to steal the necklace when he had the chance. She couldn't just take the necklace, because Kitty knew she had a key, so she provided a "suspicious" plumber.

Timing Is Everything

1) Who killed James Hooligan?

Muriel Huxley.

2) Explain the key elements of timing in this case.

First of all, the bathroom light of Hooligan's case simply burned out; it bore no relationship to the crime! (Before you cry "foul play," let me say that this little nugget came from a real case. Unlikely, but true.)

As for the method, Muriel had cut the combination lock off a couple of days before the murder, and had replaced it with an identical-looking combination lock. Her husband never realized the change had taken place, because he didn't have any occasion to get into the cabinet in the meantime. Muriel also took the rifle out at that earlier time. She killed Hooligan prior to the meeting between her husband, Martinez, and Plotz, and she ditched the rifle in the woods, just as she had ditched the bolt cutters a couple of days before. But the extra rust on the bolt cutters suggested they might have been outside longer than just one night. A fatal mistake.

A couple of other small "timing" clues pointed Muriel's way. Remember that when she came down with the news of Hooligan's death, she had just finished planting all those daffodil bulbs. But she couldn't have been planting all that long; it was still morning, and besides, she had just heard the radio announcement, which presumably had been mentioned many times on her all-news station. It follows that she had been doing her gardening for several days despite her being "locked out" of the shed, taking advantage of her husband's preoccupation with the kickback scheme.

3) What was the missing piece of evidence that tied the murderer to the crime?

The missing piece of evidence was the other lock—the one Muriel Huxley bought to replace the lock she cut off with the bolt cutters! (If you guessed the burned-out light bulb in Hooligan's bathroom, take credit for some good sleuthing.)

And just why did Muriel kill James Hooligan? Because she and her husband were getting along dreadfully, and she saw a way out of the marriage, the blackmailing, everything. She knew that her husband and/or his henchmen would be blamed for the crime, precisely because she had no apparent motive. Unfortunately for poor Muriel, she was now going to a place where someone else would hold the key to the lock.

The Churchill Letter
The letter was dated in 1950 and refers to "Sir Winston", but Churchill was not knighted (thereby earning the use of the title "Sir") until 1953.

Stanwick Visits the Golden Crown
To do the delicate safecracking required, the thief would have had to remove the thick glove on his better hand, keeping the other glove on to prevent unnecessary fingerprints. The right glove was removed for this purpose, indicating that the thief was right-handed. Johansen, however, as shown by the publican's remark on his prowess at darts, is left-handed.

Stanwick therefore correctly suspects that Johansen is being framed.

The Case of the Dubious Drowning
Stanwick observed that there was no towel or robe by the pool. Not even a hardy swimmer would normally choose to walk 60 feet from an outside pool to a house in increasingly chilly weather dripping wet. He therefore deduced that the swimming incident had been staged, and suspects—correctly, as it turned out—Mr. Duncomb.

Stanwick and the Spurious Silver Miner

In the southern hemisphere, January and February are summer months. Stanwick's visitor is plainly unaware of this, which would be an impossibility if he had just visited southern Brazil.

A Theft at the Art Museum

One of the thieves is Ed's sister, who cannot be Charlayne, an only child, and must therefore be Beverly. The other thief is either Archie or Charlayne, his wife. Douglas, who was on the scene, is neither one of the thieves nor the driver (since he can't drive), so he must be the lookout.

Ed is neither one of the thieves nor the lookout. With his long criminal record, he can't be the driver, who was first arrested less than two years ago. He is therefore the one not involved.

Charlayne, an only child, cannot be the driver, who has a brother. She must therefore be one of the thieves, and her husband Archie must be the driver.

A Mere Matter of Deduction

At least one of the three is guilty. No others were involved. If Burke is guilty, then of course he was involved. If Addington is guilty, then he must have had an accomplice (since he never works alone), but it couldn't have been Chatham, who refuses to work with him, so it must have been Burke.

Similarly, if Chatham is guilty, then he must have had an accomplice, who couldn't have been Addington, with whom he refuses to work, and so must have been Burke.

Therefore Burke must have been involved in the case.

The Prints of Lightness
1) Who killed Oscar Delahanty?

The killer was Stan Norton, with an assist (either intentional or otherwise) from Ginger LaCroix.

First of all, Norton killed Oscar Delahanty by smothering him with a pillow. It was apparent that Delahanty must have been alive when the workmen started that morning, because his windows were closed. Ordinarily those windows would have been open at night to give the room some air—as we learned in the question-and-answer session, the house, being a landmark site, would not have been permitted to have central air conditioning. The need for fresh air would have been even greater than usual because of the chemicals used by the floor refinishers. The conclusion is that Delahanty was awakened by the noise of the jackhammer (a necessary part of the hydrant installation, because underground pipes would have to be exposed). He then closed the bedroom window and went back to sleep.

It follows that the killer must have arrived sometime after the workmen started, which was at 8:30 A.M. Therefore, Mitchell Quinn couldn't have been the killer, because he had been in the salon since 8:00.

Ginger LaCroix wasn't the killer, but for a different reason. She was also going to be let go by her boss, and had also harbored thoughts of killing him. Therefore, she started the fire! (Note that she expressed concern about the condition of the house upon hearing that her boss had died of asphyxia; at that point, however, the authorities hadn't mentioned anything about a fire.) Why Norton didn't arrive at the salon until after LaCroix is anyone's guess, but clearly the strangulation occurred before the fire! Note that we don't have enough information to conclude that there was a conspiracy between Norton and LaCroix. In fact, their separate confessions suggest they weren't working in cahoots.

2) Who wrongly confessed to the crime?

Ginger LaCroix. She honestly believed that she had killed Delahanty by setting fire to his home. However, Delahanty was already dead by the time Ginger arrived, as suggested by his inability to react to the smoke alarm. Of course, Ginger wasn't completely off the hook. She still faced an arson rap, and was lucky to avoid prosecution for attempted murder!

3) How did the coroner's report help identify the killer?

The autopsy would have revealed that Delahanty did not have any soot in his lungs, as would have been expected had he actually died of smoke inhalation. (There would also have been any number of specific indications that he had been smothered, but ruling out smoke inhalation as the cause of death was the most important autopsy finding.)

4) What was the "evidence" that was destroyed?

As Norton left Delahanty's house, he left his footprints on the back steps, which were still not completely dry because of the humid weather. However, this entire area, footprints included, was destroyed in the fire. And that's a wrap.

Index

Answer pages are in italics.